Why Things Don't Work
HELICOPTER

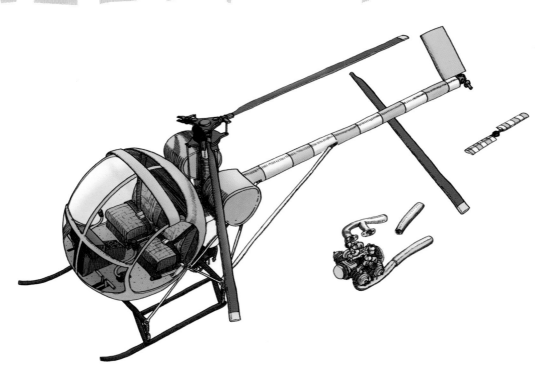

Published by Raintree, a division of Reed Elsevier, Inc.
Chicago, Illinois

Customer Service 888-363-4266
Visit our website at www.raintreelibrary.com

Why Things Don't Work HELICOPTER
was produced by

David West 👫 **Children's Books**
7 Princeton Court
55 Felsham Road
London SW15 1AZ

Editor: Dominique Crowley
Consultant: William Moore

11 10 09 08 07
10 9 8 7 6 5 4 3 2 1

Library of Congress Cataloging-in-Publication Data

West, David.
  Why things don't work. Helicopter / by David West.
    p. cm. -- (Why things don't work)
  Includes index.
  ISBN 1-4109-2558-7
  1. Helicopters--Maintenance and repair--Juvenile literature. 2.
Helicopters--Parts--Juvenile literature. I. Title. II. Title: Helicopter.
III. Series: West, David. Why things don't work.

TL716.2.W47 2007
629.133'3520288--dc22

                                              2006018088

Printed and bound in China

Why Things Don't Work
HELICOPTER

by David West

Raintree
Chicago, Illinois

Contents

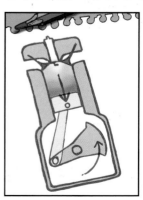

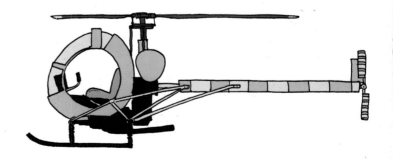

Cousin Ed's Helicopter

ANNIE HAS RECENTLY PASSED HER HELICOPTER FLYING TEST. HER COUSIN, ED, HAS AGREED TO LET HER FLY HIS HELICOPTER IF SHE HELPS HIM FIX IT. RIGHT NOW, IT IS ON HIS HELIPAD WITH NO FUEL IN THE TANK.

ALSO, THERE SEEM TO BE A FEW OTHER PROBLEMS...

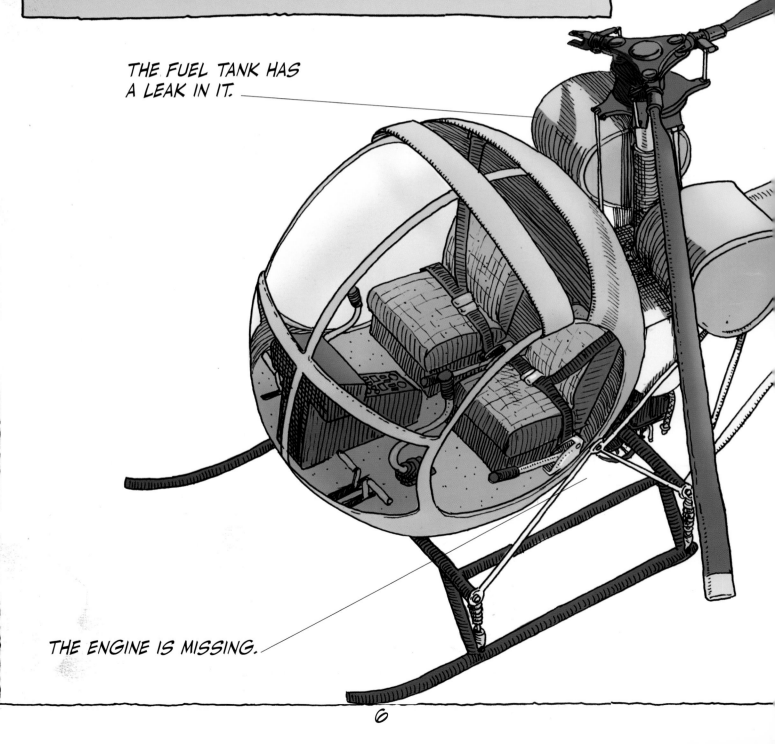

THE FUEL TANK HAS A LEAK IN IT.

THE ENGINE IS MISSING.

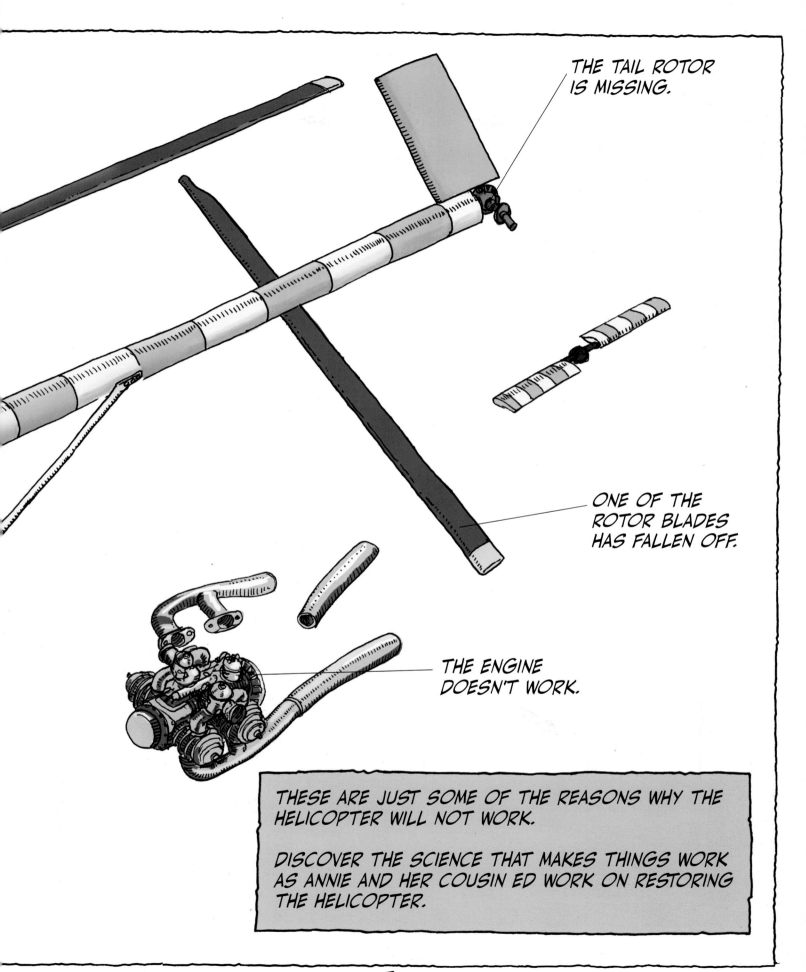

THE TAIL ROTOR IS MISSING.

ONE OF THE ROTOR BLADES HAS FALLEN OFF.

THE ENGINE DOESN'T WORK.

THESE ARE JUST SOME OF THE REASONS WHY THE HELICOPTER WILL NOT WORK.

DISCOVER THE SCIENCE THAT MAKES THINGS WORK AS ANNIE AND HER COUSIN ED WORK ON RESTORING THE HELICOPTER.

WELL, HERE IT IS.

WOW! WHAT HAPPENED TO IT?

IT GOT KNOCKED OVER IN HIGH WINDS A FEW MONTHS AGO. WE HAVEN'T HAD TIME TO REPAIR IT UNTIL NOW.

THE ENGINE SEEMS TO BE MISSING!

I'VE GOT IT OVER HERE ON THE WORK BENCH.

IT'S A FLAT FOUR PISTON ENGINE.

WHAT'S A FLAT FOUR PISTON ENGINE?

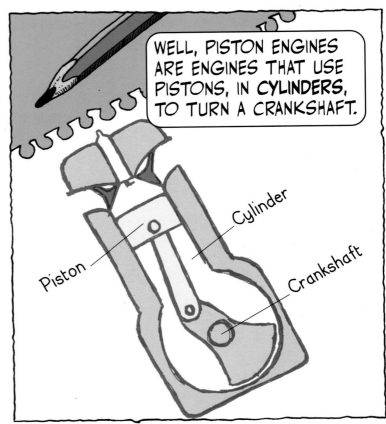

WELL, PISTON ENGINES ARE ENGINES THAT USE PISTONS, IN **CYLINDERS**, TO TURN A CRANKSHAFT.

Piston

Cylinder

Crankshaft

IN A NORMAL ENGINE, THERE ARE USUALLY FOUR CYLINDERS ARRANGED IN A LINE.

SOME ENGINE DESIGNS HAVE THE CYLINDERS ARRANGED IN A V-SHAPE. AND SOME HAVE SIX, EIGHT, TEN, OR EVEN TWELVE CYLINDERS.

IN A FLAT FOUR THERE ARE FOUR CYLINDERS THAT ARE LYING DOWN.

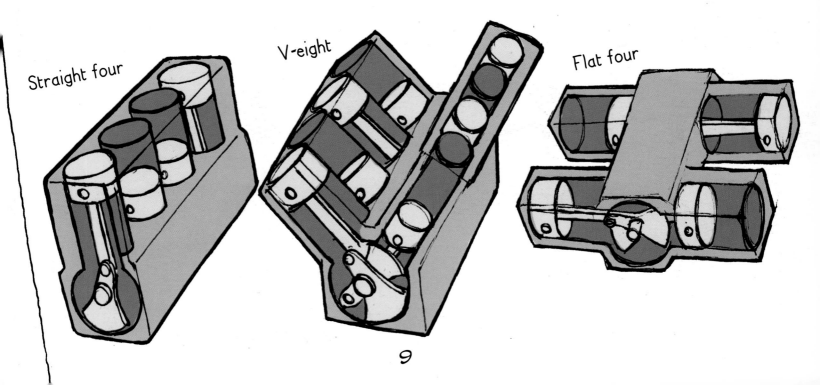

Straight four

V-eight

Flat four

FUEL AND AIR ARE SUCKED INTO THE **COMBUSTION CHAMBER** AS THE PISTON MOVES DOWN.

Fuel and air mix enters cylinder from **carburetor**.

AS THE PISTON MOVES UP, IT SQUEEZES THE AIR/FUEL MIXTURE.

Fuel and air mix is squashed.

A **SPARK PLUG** CAUSES THE AIR/FUEL MIXTURE TO EXPLODE, FORCING THE PISTON DOWN.

A spark from the spark plug makes the fuel and air mixture explode.

Exhaust gases are forced out.

WHEN THE PISTON RETURNS, IT FORCES THE **EXHAUST GASES** OUT. THEN THE WHOLE PROCESS STARTS AGAIN.

EXCEPT, IN THIS CASE, IT DOESN'T. LOOK AT THAT. THE OIL HAS LEAKED OUT FROM A CRACK AND THE WHOLE ENGINE HAS SEIZED UP.

WHY?

OIL MAKES THE SURFACES OF THE MOVING PARTS SLIPPERY. THIS HELPS REDUCE FRICTION, WHICH CREATES A LOT OF HEAT.

RUB YOUR HANDS TOGETHER. CAN YOU FEEL THE HEAT BUILD UP?

YES.

THAT'S WHAT HAPPENED TO THIS ENGINE. IT GOT SO HOT, THE PARTS OVERHEATED AND JAMMED. THIS BROKE THE ENGINE.

11

CAN IT BE REPAIRED?

NO. IT'S TOO BADLY DAMAGED.

LUCKILY, I GOT THIS FROM A SCRAPYARD. IT'S A WANKEL ROTARY ENGINE.

WOW. HOW MANY CYLINDERS DOES IT HAVE?

IT DOESN'T HAVE ANY CYLINDERS! IT WORKS DIFFERENTLY FROM A PISTON ENGINE.

SEE THIS TRIANGULAR PART? THIS SPINS AROUND. THERE ARE NO PARTS GOING UP AND DOWN AS IN PISTON ENGINES.

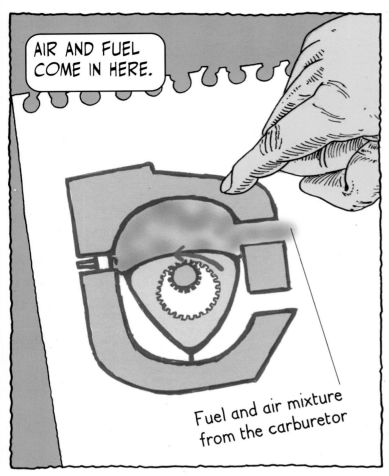

AIR AND FUEL COME IN HERE.

Fuel and air mixture from the carburetor

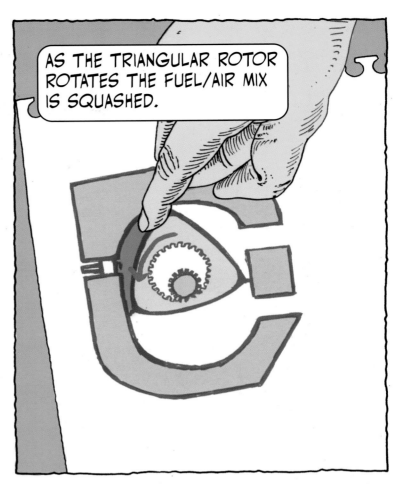

AS THE TRIANGULAR ROTOR ROTATES THE FUEL/AIR MIX IS SQUASHED.

THE SPARK PLUG **IGNITES** THE FUEL/AIR MIX, WITH A SPARK. THE EXPLODING GASES EXPAND, FORCING THE TRIANGLE AROUND.

Spark plug

THE EXHAUST GASES ARE PUSHED OUT HERE.

Exhaust gases

THE SAME THING HAPPENS IN THE OTHER THREE SPACES.

THE ROTATING TRIANGLE TURNS A SHAFT IN THE MIDDLE. THIS PROVIDES THE TURNING FORCE.

Rotating shaft

AS YOU CAN SEE, IT HAS FEWER MOVING PARTS THAN A PISTON ENGINE. THIS MAKES THE WHOLE THING MUCH LIGHTER.

WE PUT THE ENGINE BACK TOGETHER AND ATTACHED IT TO THE HELICOPTER.

LOOK. ONE OF THE ROTOR BLADES HAS FALLEN OFF.

YES. THAT'S THE NEXT THING WE NEED TO FIX.

WHICH WAY UP DOES IT GO?

THIS WAY. IT'S JUST LIKE A PLANE'S WING.

Lift

Low air pressure area

Faster moving air

Rotor blade **cross-section**

Slower moving air

AS THE BLADE TURNS, THE AIR RUSHING OVER THE TOP SURFACE GOES FASTER, BECAUSE IT HAS FARTHER TO TRAVEL THAN THE AIR TRAVELING UNDERNEATH.

THIS CREATES AN AREA OF **LOW AIR PRESSURE** ABOVE THE BLADE. THE BLADE MOVES INTO THIS AREA, PULLING THE REST OF THE HELICOPTER WITH IT.

TO SEE HOW THIS WORKS, IMAGINE THIS PIECE OF PAPER IS THE CURVED EDGE OF A WING.

WHEN I BLOW OVER THE TOP, THE SPEEDING AIR SHOULD MAKE IT LIFT UP.

WOW!

15

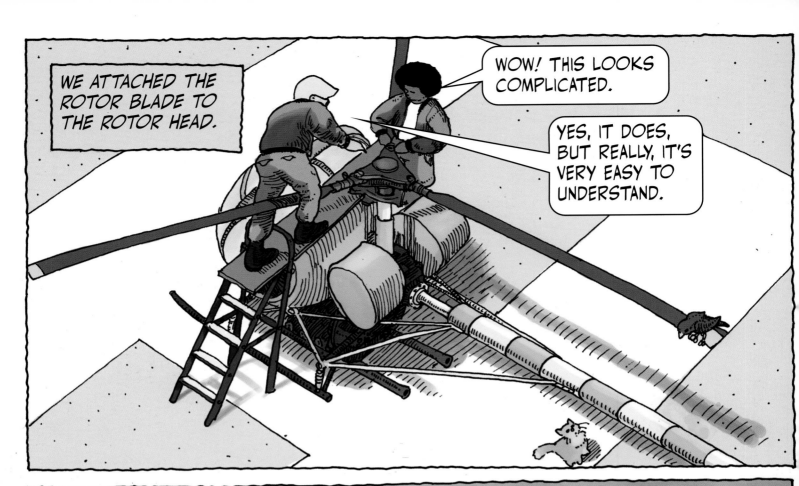

THAT'S RIGHT. AS THE SWASH PLATE MOVES, IT PUSHES THESE **PITCH ARM RODS** UP OR DOWN.

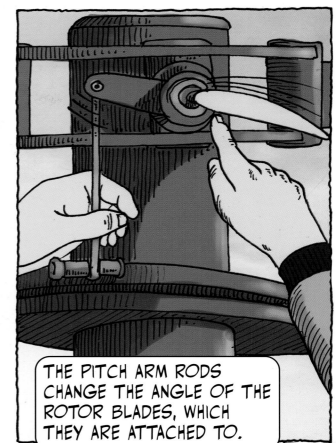

THE PITCH ARM RODS CHANGE THE ANGLE OF THE ROTOR BLADES, WHICH THEY ARE ATTACHED TO.

WHAT DOES THAT DO?

THE STEEPER THE BLADE'S ANGLE, THE MORE LIFT IT PROVIDES.

THIS MEANS YOU CAN TILT THE HELICOPTER IN ANY DIRECTION BY TILTING THE SWASH PLATE.

Helicopter tilts left.

More lift

Blade faces up.

Helicopter tilts forwards.

Negative lift

Blade faces down.

17

IF THE WHOLE SWASH PLATE IS RAISED, ALL THE BLADES TWIST AT THE SAME ANGLE. THIS WILL CREATE LIFT ON ALL THE BLADES AT THE SAME TIME...

...WHICH MAKES THE HELICOPTER GO STRAIGHT UP.

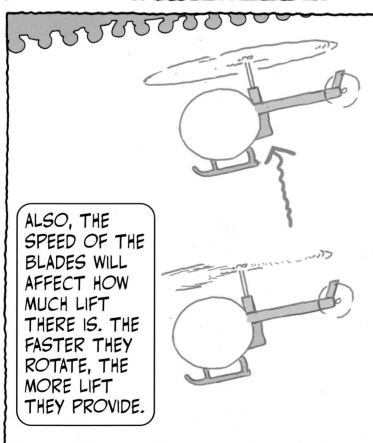

ALSO, THE SPEED OF THE BLADES WILL AFFECT HOW MUCH LIFT THERE IS. THE FASTER THEY ROTATE, THE MORE LIFT THEY PROVIDE.

THE BLADES FEEL A BIT WOBBLY.

YES, THEY'RE MEANT TO.

THE BLADES ACTUALLY BEND AS THEY ROTATE. THIS SOLVES A PROBLEM YOU WOULD GET IF THEY WERE RIGID.

IN ORDER TO STOP THIS, THE BLADES GOING FORWARD BEND UP, WHICH REDUCES THEIR LIFT.

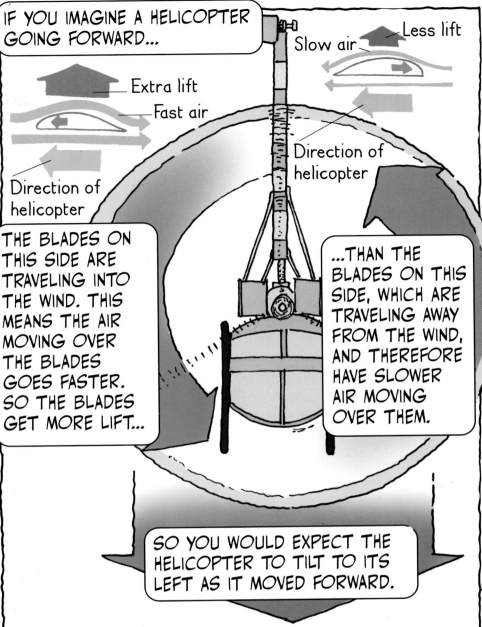

IF YOU IMAGINE A HELICOPTER GOING FORWARD...

Extra lift

Fast air

Direction of helicopter

Less lift

Slow air

Direction of helicopter

THE BLADES ON THIS SIDE ARE TRAVELING INTO THE WIND. THIS MEANS THE AIR MOVING OVER THE BLADES GOES FASTER. SO THE BLADES GET MORE LIFT...

...THAN THE BLADES ON THIS SIDE, WHICH ARE TRAVELING AWAY FROM THE WIND, AND THEREFORE HAVE SLOWER AIR MOVING OVER THEM.

SO YOU WOULD EXPECT THE HELICOPTER TO TILT TO ITS LEFT AS IT MOVED FORWARD.

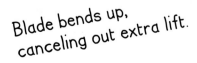

Blade bends up, canceling out extra lift.

Blade bends down, which creates more lift.

THE BLADES GOING BACKWARD BEND DOWN LIKE A BIRD'S WING, WHICH CREATES EXTRA LIFT. THIS EVENS OUT ANY DIFFERENCE IN AIR SPEED OVER THE ROTOR BLADES.

OH DEAR. HERE'S OUR PROBLEM. THERE'S NO TAIL ROTOR.

WHAT DOES IT DO?

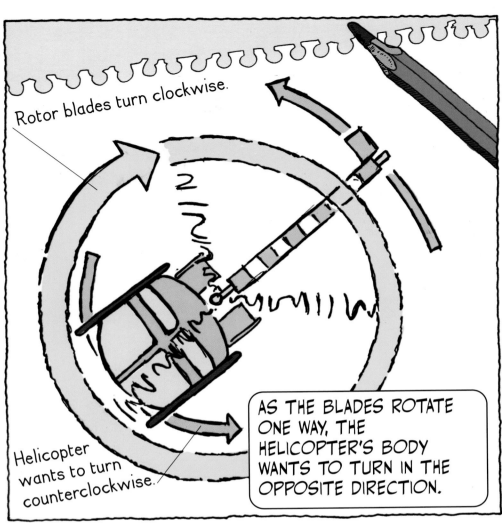

Rotor blades turn clockwise.

Helicopter wants to turn counterclockwise.

AS THE BLADES ROTATE ONE WAY, THE HELICOPTER'S BODY WANTS TO TURN IN THE OPPOSITE DIRECTION.

SIT IN THIS SWIVEL CHAIR AND TRY TO SPIN AROUND WITHOUT TOUCHING ANYTHING.

WHOA.

YOU SEE, AS YOUR TOP HALF WANTS TO GO ONE WAY, THE BOTTOM HALF WANTS TO GO THE OTHER WAY.

THIS IS WHAT HAPPENS TO A HELICOPTER WITHOUT A TAIL ROTOR.

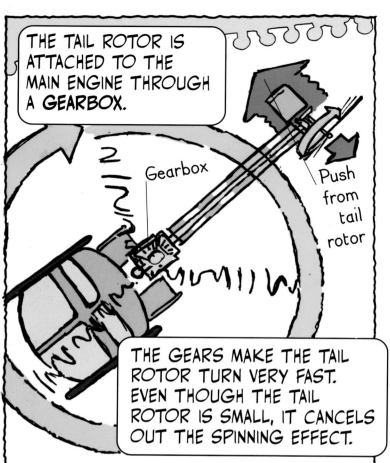

THE TAIL ROTOR IS ATTACHED TO THE MAIN ENGINE THROUGH A **GEARBOX**.

Gearbox

Push from tail rotor

THE GEARS MAKE THE TAIL ROTOR TURN VERY FAST. EVEN THOUGH THE TAIL ROTOR IS SMALL, IT CANCELS OUT THE SPINNING EFFECT.

WE ATTACHED THE TAIL ROTOR ONTO ITS **AXLE** AT THE END.

I'LL JUST GO AND CLEAN UP AND THEN WE'LL TAKE THE HELICOPTER OUT FOR A TEST FLIGHT.

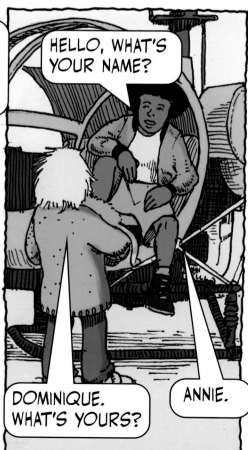

HELLO, WHAT'S YOUR NAME?

DOMINIQUE. WHAT'S YOURS?

ANNIE.

ARE YOU GOING TO FLY ED'S HELICOPTER?

YES.

WHAT ARE THOSE STICKS FOR?

THIS IS CALLED THE CYCLIC CONTROL STICK. IT MAKES THE HELICOPTER GO FORWARD, BACKWARD, OR SIDEWAYS. SEE HOW IT MOVES THE SWASH PLATE?

THIS ONE IS CALLED THE PITCH CONTROL LEVER. IT MAKES THE HELICOPTER GO UP AND DOWN BY MOVING THE SWASH PLATE UP AND DOWN. IT ALSO HAS THE **THROTTLE** CONTROL ON IT, TO MAKE THE BLADES TURN FASTER.

THE PEDALS, HERE, CHANGE THE ANGLE OF THE TAIL ROTOR BLADES. THEY MAKE THE HELICOPTER POINT LEFT OR RIGHT.

23

HI, DOMINIQUE. YOU'D BETTER GO INSIDE. WE'RE GOING ON A TEST FLIGHT.

CAN I COME?

WE NEED TO TEST IT FIRST. YOU CAN COME NEXT TIME.

OK. BYE ANNIE.

OK. READY WHEN YOU ARE.

WEEEEEEEEEEE
WHUP
WHUP

TWIST THE THROTTLE FOR MORE POWER AND LIFT THE PITCH CONTROL LEVER.

WHUPPA WHUPPA WHUPPA

WHUPPA
WHUPPA
WHUPPA

LET DOWN THE PITCH CONTROL LEVER A BIT TO STOP CLIMBING.

WHUPPA
WHUPPA
WHUPPA

PUSH THE CYCLIC CONTROL LEVER FORWARD AND LIFT THE PITCH CONTROL LEVER.

WE MOVED FORWARD.

I PUSHED THE LEFT FOOT PEDAL TO POINT WEST AND PULLED THE PITCH CONTROL LEVER TO GAIN HEIGHT.

WHUPPA

WHUPPA

WHUPPA

26

I TRIED TO REMEMBER EMERGENCY PROCEDURE FROM MY LESSONS, PUTTING US INTO A DIVE. THE AIR RACING OVER THE BLADES KEPT THEM ROTATING.

SWISH SWISH SWISH

THAT FIELD LOOKS GOOD TO LAND IN.

JUST BEFORE WE HIT THE GROUND I PULLED UP THE NOSE USING THE PITCH CONTROL LEVER AND THE CYCLIC CONTROL STICK.

HOLD ON!

THE FREELY ROTATING BLADES CREATED ENOUGH LIFT FOR THE HELICOPTER TO SLOW TO NORMAL LANDING SPEED.

SWISH SWISH

WE LANDED WITH A FAINT BUMP.

SWISH SWISH

NICE LANDING.

27

IT TURNED OUT THERE WAS A LEAK IN THE FUEL TANK. WE SOON HAD IT PATCHED UP AND, THE FOLLOWING WEEK, WE FLEW TO AN AIR SHOW IN THE HELICOPTER.

WHUPPA

WHUPPA

WHUPPA

WE SAW A TWIN-ROTOR HELICOPTER CALLED A CHINOOK.

HEY, THAT HELICOPTER HAS NO TAIL ROTOR.

IT DOESN'T NEED ONE. THE SECOND ROTOR ROTATES IN THE OPPOSITE DIRECTION WHICH HAS THE SAME EFFECT.

LOOK, THIS ONE DOES THE SAME THING BUT ONE ROTOR SITS ABOVE THE OTHER.

I'M NOT SURE IF I'D WANT TO DO THAT.

THEY HAVE TO IF THEY ARE RESCUING SOMEONE AT SEA.

28

THERE WAS A HUGE RUSSIAN GUNSHIP...

IT'S CALLED A HIND.

...AND AN AMAZING DISPLAY BY AN APACHE HELICOPTER.

WOW! IT CAN DO A LOOP.

WE SAW A CROSS BETWEEN A PLANE AND A HELICOPTER. THE ENGINES TILTED UPWARD SO IT COULD TAKE OFF AND LAND VERTICALLY.

IT'S CALLED AN OSPREY.

THE BEST BIT WAS HAVING A RIDE IN A GYROCOPTER. IT HAD A PROPELLER TO POWER IT, BUT THE ROTOR JUST TURNED FREELY TO GIVE LIFT.

IT FLIES JUST LIKE OUR HELICOPTER DID WHEN WE HAD THE EMERGENCY.

29

Parts of a Helicopter

Rotor head

Rotor blades

Cockpit

Swash plate

Tail rotor

Fuel tank

Cyclic control stick

Gearbox

Engine

Pitch control lever

Tail rotor

Rotor head

Rotor blades

Swash plate

Instrument panel

Cyclic control sticks

Fuel tanks

Rotor head

Instrument panel

Pedals

Cyclic control sticks

Rotor blades

Glossary

AXLE
A METAL ROD OR PIN ON WHICH A
SPINNING OBJECT SUCH AS A WHEEL OR
ROTOR BLADE IS ATTACHED

CARBURETOR
PART OF AN ENGINE THAT MIXES FUEL AND
AIR TOGETHER BEFORE THEY ENTER THE
COMBUSTION CHAMBER

COMBUSTION CHAMBER
TOP PART OF THE CYLINDER WHERE THE
FUEL/AIR MIXTURE IS IGNITED BY THE
SPARK PLUG

CROSS-SECTION
THE SHAPE SHOWN OF AN OBJECT WHEN
IT IS SLICED THROUGH BY AN
MAGINARY BLADE

CYLINDER
THE METAL SLEEVE INSIDE WHICH A
PISTON MOVES

EXHAUST GASES
FUMES THAT ARE CREATED BY THE
EXPLODING FUEL/AIR MIXTURE IN
THE ENGINE

FRICTION
THE RESISTANCE MET BY TWO SURFACES
RUBBING AGAINST EACH OTHER

FUEL
A LIQUID FROM OIL THAT BURNS
VIOLENTLY WHEN IGNITED

GEARBOX
THE HOUSING FOR THE GEARS

IGNITE
TO SET ON FIRE

LOW AIR PRESSURE AREA
AN AREA OF AIR THAT HAS LESS AIR THAN
ITS SURROUNDING AREA

PISTON
A METAL CYLINDER THAT MOVES BACK AND
FORTH INSIDE ANOTHER CYLINDER

PITCH ARM ROD
A METAL ROD ATTACHED BY JOINTS TO
THE SWASH PLATE AND THE ROTOR BLADE.
AS IT MOVES UP OR DOWN, IT CHANGES
THE PITCH, OR ANGLE, OF THE
ROTOR BLADE.

RIGID
FIRM AND INFLEXIBLE

ROTATE
TURNING MOTION

SPARK PLUG
A PART IN THE TOP OF AN ENGINE'S
CYLINDER THAT CREATES AN ELECTRIC
SPARK TO IGNITE THE FUEL/AIR MIXTURE

SWASH PLATE
TWO LARGE METAL DISCS, ONE ON TOP
OF THE OTHER, BELOW THE ROTOR HEAD

THROTTLE
A DEVICE THAT CONTROLS THE AMOUNT
OF FUEL GOING INTO THE ENGINE, AND
THEREFORE HOW FAST OR SLOW IT
WILL GO

Index